Stranger
to
the
Beautiful

Stranger to the Beautiful

Don Hynes

Library of Congress Cataloging In Publication Data
Names: Hynes, Don—author
Title: Stranger to the Beautiful
Description: Portland, Oregon : Slender Arrow Press
Identifiers: LCCN — applied for, TBD

ISBN: 978-0-9741648-3-0 (paperback)
ISBN: 978-0-9741648-4-7 (ebook)

For more information contact:
Slender Arrow Press
429 NE 29th Ave.
Portland OR 97232

Photography by Dennis Brown, Sandy Brown Jensen, Ann Foorman, Louis MacKenzie, Linda Ethier

Cover photo by Sandy Brown Jensen
Book Design by: Abbey Gregory

Also by Don Hynes

Slender Arrow
Out From Under
The Living Dark
The Irish Girl
Something Will Change Me

Contents

*The earth opens
and down I tumble,
into a vault of seeds,
perfect and unbroken.*

Introduction

To read Don Hynes is to encounter a voice that has become synonymous with the spirit of the Pacific Northwest. While many poets pass through these moss-draped forests and rugged coastlines, few have inhabited them with the sustained, soulful attention that Don has offered over the course of five volumes—from *Slender Arrow* to *Something Will Change Me*—and decades of weekly devotion in his *Poet's Journal.* He stands today as a primary architect of our regional consciousness, a poet whose work does not merely describe our landscape but emerges from it as a vital "sky map" for the inner life.

Don's lineage is one of deep presence and structural integrity. He belongs to that rare class of poets who understand that "the weight of winter" is far more than a season; it is a profound metaphorical state of the world. In these pages, winter is the "dark chamber" of the human collective, a repository of error and "careless words" where we must learn to "excavate joy" even when the dawns are wet and gray. His poems carry the weight of a man who spent a career building physical foundations for the community and now, in these "autumn years," builds the spiritual scaffolding we need to withstand the cold.

In *Stranger to the Beautiful*, we see a master at the height of his powers, one who has allowed the "wildness" of existence to drive out arrogance. He is our witness on the "yearning shore," reminding us that even when the world feels shrouded in "desperate folly," we are not lost. He teaches us a way of communion that requires no chanting or spells—only "one simple yes" to the wonders that persist despite the darkness.

Don Hynes is more than a poet of our generation; he is a keeper of the "hidden stone," the birthplace of beauty. He reminds us that even as the cultural landscape seems to "descend," we have the "stars in flight" to guide us. He proves, through every carefully chosen word, that we are "children of the eternal," and that even in the deepest frost of the soul, we are good.

—Sandy Brown Jensen

Weight of Winter

Solstice Ladder

Down the solstice ladder
to the crib where phantoms dwell,
wearing the guise of ancient familiars
who cut and tear, heartless
in the gloom.

I won't save these ghosts,
but in the night-work
soulful needles pierce the lie,
threads of compassion
draw together the riven cloth.

Welcome the dark chamber,
the repository of error.
Where careless words
and bitter feelings burn
upon the yuletide fire;

come now the return of light.

Stranger to the Beautiful

Dropping like rain,
I fall into a new year
of starless nights,
wet gray dawns.

As crows return
to evergreen silence
I search and shovel
to excavate joy.

The earth opens
and down I tumble,
into a vault of seeds,
perfect and unbroken.

The goddess of night
protects these treasures,
and stranger to the beautiful
I fall in love

with moonless
winter sleeping.

Welcome

Welcome darkness,
fear and blight,
welcome suffering,
welcome night.

Welcome the beautiful,
desert and seas,
welcome the mountains,
welcome the trees.

Welcome ignorance,
violence and pain,
welcome the homeless,
welcome the rain.

Welcome the thoughtful
giver of gifts,
welcome the lame,
welcome the swift.

Welcome the womb,
seed and flower,
welcome the timeless,
welcome the hour.

Welcome the grieving,
all who mourn,
welcome the earth,
welcome the dawn.

God's Idea

In the quiet dark
earth nurtures her future
below cold wet ground.

Forests wait in embryo—
plants, flowers, the vastness
of green to come,
alive in the winter womb,
fed by her heartbeat.

My undiscovered self
waits also for the spark,
for God's idea
of who I might be
when I rise into light.

Weight of Winter

I rise and fall
the ancient way,
from root to leaf
and back to earth;
the road I tread
these autumn years,
without desire
or fear of death.

Gone with summer
the need to shine,
I seek the earth
like fallen leaves.
Birds fly high,
owl hunts night,
my wings fold
as deep roots call.

Released one winter
from weight of snow
and what must pass,
to lift and go
a weathered hawk—
dark-night stars
to guide me.

Who Dare to Sing

Drunk on starlight
I stumble in the temple,
loud in praise
of Aldebaran and Sirius.

I never will be sober
while desire guides me,
lured by darkness
to distant light,

where sky gods celebrate
those who love night glory,
who dare once more
to sing among the stars.

Taking Flight

Snow-covered hills
under winter's blanket,
I wake in a foreign land
with trees of ash and oak,
bare branched like veins
in the gray sky.

However far I travel
the earth remains the earth,
held like a newborn
each new day,
a silent presence
among the stars.

The gift of light,
the mystery of the deep,
and everywhere she rises
in the age-old prayer
of becoming.

Let me too be lifted
from the creek beds
of the unconscious,
to find myself
adorned with wings
in the Catskill mountains
of imagination.

Silence of the Mountains

Into the quiet dark
I commit my messengers,
the sole survivors
of desperate folly.

Carry word
to the wanderers;
they must hear
of the rising stars
unseen before this night.

The sky map
will guide them
beyond the desert
of uncertainty,

to the river
of crystal water,
where tablets of the future
are written in green.

May the silence
of the mountains
be their comfort.

Hidden Stone

I shelter with trees
below cold wet ground,
what's left above
leafless, without color.

Burrowing in soft earth,
I find roots of peace
woven to the hidden stone,
birthplace of beauty.

There She holds me,
child in Her lap,
cradled once more
in Her undying Eden.

Slow Down

When snow covers the valley
the time is here to slow down,

to let earth's winter rhythm
seep into the deep-celled longing
of the body for peace,

and a place of home
within the great silence.

Secrets of the Dawn

The slow light of morning
slips into awakening
with secrets of the dawn,

of silence stored in mountain caves
lined with walls of ice,

flowing now like a river,
in the rise of springtime song.

Give Your Hand

> Quiet the restless mind,
> still the surge of emotion.
>
> Let this hour belong
> to the One who grants the gift.
>
> Leave the drunkards at their bar,
> your hand given to the Beloved.

Armies of the Angel

Dragons of the defiled mind
roar against spring tree flowers,
breathe fire upon the sleeping.

Death, death it is,
their horrid voices croak,
as mountain rivers melt
in rushing floods.

Yet even as waters boil,
deep within the earth
armies of the Angel rise,
trumpeting symphonies
of the apocalypse.

Water on Stone

Choirs of Earth

Pulled from the morass,
I see evergreens in the distance
and messages of earth alive,
in blooms of the plum tree.

Quiet before the mystery,
I hear voices behind the clouds,
light shimmering
in the soft breaks of morning.

With few years left,
I carve prayers of thanks
on stone faces
of the unforgiving,

for the choirs of earth
to raise in song.

Dark Comfort

Warm before the fire
I watch trees flower
and gray valley skies
soften in growing light.

Neither cold nor hot
in the changing time,
winter still clings
to mountain slopes,
lowlands burgeon
with the weight of color.

Willows lend courage
as red birds call,
to leave dark comfort
and rise in earth glory.

Easter

Bring me day
in sunlit glory,
vital earth
and flowing tide.

Bring me night,
moonlit haunting,
cry of owls
and stars in flight.

Bring me peace
to heal the soul,
balm of silence
soothe my heart.

Bring me life
beyond all faith,
your gift, dear One,
in morning light.

Water on Stone

Tracking my years
like water on stone—

drip.. drip.. drip..
as the hardest places
dissolve to sand

and stone opens
to the light beyond.

Druids' Signal

Hidden by noise
the druids' signal,
messages of rebirth
within chaos.

From the dark-night forest
and fortresses of grace,
on hummingbird wings
and raven's croak,

their signal rises,
drawing up spring beauty
to shock the world
into consciousness.

If You Hear Me

Dark night beauty,
densely clouded skies;
rain showers the metal roof.

I rest in comfort,
alien to bright lights
and discordant sound,
here where grasses wave,
leaves speak in trees,

and broadcast from the borderland
to the animal within you—
wild for the wind and sea.

Signal the stars if you hear me,
and lift your soul in silence steeped,

that dark night beauty might find you.

Evening Quiet

Silent as the earth
I match her pace,
steady and serene
in evening quiet.

Why conjure problems
while swallows perform,
and the world is bathed in light?

Eye to Eye

Sitting in silence,
thoughts flow with the tide,
as nameless waters,
broad to the horizon,
lift and fall.

Iris' rise in spring sun,
their color purple,
while I study the depths
of moss and April flower,

shortening my sight
to the near at hand,
eye to eye with the Creator.

Silence Falls

Slack tide seas
mope about,
then silence falls,
a welcome blanket.

The lure of deep water
and gathering night,
held in the mystery

I kneel to taste
at the earth altar.

Softening Stone *(for Ann)*

Silent and beautiful,
the artful earth
in rising green
and silver sea.

I drink the free air
and let her beauty
soak my innards,

softening stone
to morning milk.

Children of the Eternal

I train my eyes upon the living sea,
rise and fall and waves of wind,

then look upon swaying grass,
gone to seed with shades of brown.

Sees-far mountains rim the coast,
trees tower in silence,

bird songs flit about
ocean spray and Nootka rose.

Sunlight heals the eyes,
water sounds a listening grace.

Lineage of sun and earth,
children of the eternal,

here and now, we are good.

Where Tide Meets Wind

Winds pick up,
and trouble the sea—
clouds lower the sky.

Where tide meets wind
the sea rolls in waves,
as thought follows feeling.

Silence sharpens the mind,
stillness quiets the heart.

Focused like a tree,
I gather the earth within,
and silently I rise.

Hymns of Praise

Wonder's threshold,
with depths uncharted
and horizons vast,

forgotten to many
the hymns of praise,
whispers of worship.

Yet in quiet hours
they stir my soul,
ceaseless as the sea.

Goddess Whispers

Tides of Eden

The day arrives in sunlit glory—
snow-capped mountains,
landscapes rich with color,
tidal seas chase the moon.

After years of toil and grief
I turn and face forward
in my unexpected seat
on the train to Eden.

Without pause for doubt
I fill my lungs with salt-laced air,
and my heart with the peace
of open water.

Hallowed Ground

Holy night
in quiet darkness,
half-moon glimmers,
lapping tide.

Wind drift,
wave tossed,
traces of fear dissolve
as water guides.

Spirit rises
as my heart opens,
a weightless freedom
with soul unbound.

Sunlit morning
in sacred landscape,
green leaves flutter
on hallowed ground.

Altar of the Heart

The moon in pale brilliance
brightens the summer sea,
the blessed land in silent prayer
with lilting breath of all that lives.

Upon the altar of the heart,
cleansed of conflict,
the world rests radiant
in naked splendor.

This night, blessed with song,
sings praise to the sky dome,
while benedictions of the living
bathe the earth in light.

Searching the Sky

Day breaks, sun-cast color
on a wind-rippled sea.

Crows chatter and call,
geese stir the quiet.

The world wakes
to bird sound
and shimmering light,

as I reach into the morning
like a skyward tree.

Silent Joy

First light breaks,
as winds rise
to rustle the sea.

The sun sings "awake!"
and over the broad expanse,
life stirs in its deep green bed.

Awakening, I turn over
to the sound of crows
and surging tide.

My silent joy
spills across the earth,
like waves of grass,

alive with breath
this tender dawn,
awake as a bird
in wonder.

Written on Water *(for Humphrey)*

Along the rugged shore
broken faces of old stones,
full of ancient records
and passages of the sun.

I hear their heartbeats
in cold water silence,
the passing of years
in vanished voices.

Written on water,
their stories given to the sea,
carried where tides travel
to the holy book
at the end of time.

Goddess Whispers

The swelling windless tide
eases into the cove,
to quench the gravel beach
in a slow languid laze.

Seagrass barely stirs,
even the crows are quiet,
as the sun kisses down
on the driftwood earth.

"Don't hurry from your perch,"
the Goddess whispers,
"savor the warmth
on the old sleeping rocks,"

as She spreads Her summer dress
across the shimmering water,
holding the land and sea
in saltwater embrace.

What Began With Light

Cloud breaks reveal the moon
as light spills across the water,
rousing the land and sea.

Old roots stir, ancient trees,
and stone canyons
find their voices.

Island folk emerge
from shelter
as whale song fills
the saltwater evening.

What began with light
is renewed in radiance,
and from sea depth and cavern
rise the breath of earth's joy.

On the Yearning Shore

In the quiet hours
between night and day,
the earth turns
to the coming dawn.

First light
ruffles the water,
lying still beneath
night's blanket.

I rise from bed,
stirred by the glow
of golden light
crossing the sea,

to the green land
of my soul, wakeful
on the yearning shore.

Morning Worship

In the hours of first light,
sky soft rose then sherbet orange,
tide returns to the hollows;

seals bark, otters quietly swim,
gulls cry with plaintive voices,
the world anew, without flaw.

Geese fly low over the water,
light swells, weaving its mystery,
urging the sea and sky to awaken—
the cathedral of beauty

with stained glass of brilliant hue,
wisps of cloud on vaulted ceiling,
gathering all who will
to morning worship.

Given to Silence

Sunlit summer morning,
soft air, gentle winds,
sea spread tablecloth smooth.

I breathe the air,
absorb the healing light;

and with quiet heart
given to silence,
I'm surrounded by heaven.

One Simple Yes

Before a wall
of ancient stone,
I place prayers
in cracks of silence.

As tears soften
the rough-hewn rock,
I trace a portal,
barred by tradition.

No incantations
or chanted spells,
just one simple yes
unlocks the door—

to heart's chapel,
adorned with quiet,
face to face
with the Eternal.

One Love

Ebbing seas weave between the islands
in stone valleys of ancient quiet;
gnarled trees reach for light,
stillness spreads on the rugged shore.

I sip the sea's calm peace,
breathe in the cool salt air,
while earth begins the autumn path
of letting go and renewal.

Friendships wax and wane,
tides risc and fall away,
yet in my soul's deepest core
one love lives unchanging.

After the Rain

Day of Grace

Wind freshened,
steeped in October rain,
the dry land opens
to autumn's blessing.

I search my soul
for burdens I preserve,
curses I repeat
on this day of grace.

Rooted like a tree,
I drink deep
the waters of forgiveness,
letting my soul rise
on wings of new life.

Autumn Tale

Autumn drapes the coast
with rain and heavy cloud.

The yielding land,
eased by cool air, drinks
the sky's soft blessing.

I feel the rootward pull
with daylight fading,
evening drawing close.

Nurtured by the dark,
my soul embraces night
in dreamlike mystery,

while I sew an autumn tale,
threaded with the ebbing tide,
woven by the sea.

Savor the Tide

At sunup, a line of geese
feed on the ebbing sea,
soaked in light.

With each new day
of God's imagination,

I lay an offering
of pilgrim praise
upon the earth altar.

Bowing to the eternal
like a lone goose
in boundless beauty,

I savor the tide.

Turning to Earth

Morning wind,
white-capped waves,

autumn hues—
brown and pale green,
turning to earth.

Heart sprung open
by wind and color.

Way of Communion

The world unfolds,
wind, tide and rain-soaked,
life force streaming.

Doors of imagination
swing on ancient hinges,
opening toward the Maker.

No kneeling
or supplication—
upright and sentient
before pure Intent.

Communion found
after years' of journey,
soft and supple
as tender green grass.

Rootward

Clouds lower,
geese cry,
tide rushes.

Eagle flies,
sky arrow,
daylight wanes.

Root descends,
trees pulse,
autumn falls.

Soul settles,
rain-soft earth,
dark comfort.

Stranger to the Beautiful

After the Rain

Never so bright
as after storms,
sun like fire on the sea,

ablaze with the truth
of earth made whole
again and again,

to the delight
of unseen gods.

Blind Optimist

Old age drove the arrogance out,
humbled me with aching joints,
muscles that struggle to work.

I get by — climb a hill,
carry bundles, cans of gas,
whatever the island demands,

but put me in a chair
for more than an hour
and I'm bent like an aged farmer.

What broke me was wildness,
and wildness my salvation.
I'd never have known you

if I hadn't been the blind optimist,
to ring your doorbell and sink
into your sea-green eyes.

So I put up with faltering step,
for I still have sight,
and I do see you.

Watching Like Crow

Fall winds stripped the trees,
their summer finery
burned in wet heaps.

The sun, far south,
burns orange in the roar
of roaming garbage trucks.

I gather myself
with no sight of the sea,
no scent of tide,

watching the town wake
like a rooftop crow,

at peace
above the wandering
and forgotten.

Night's Gift

As the world sleeps,
night rivers flow.

Ravenous for knowledge
I devour the silence,

then kneel, an acolyte,
in dawn's gray light,

bearing gifts of darkness.

Uprising

Night winds rouse
the old earth gods—

rivers don't sleep,
dark forests rise,

sodden roots shatter
the concrete prison.

Carry Me Down

Stirred by inner fire
dark does not frighten,
nor gray light of winter.

Carry me down
to the deepest root,
upend every truth.

Flood of spirit
scour my heart.
I'm not too old to live.

Quiet Descent

Unburdened by night,
freed of phantoms,

I wake in gray dawn
to the river-sound of traffic.

Earth muted in descent,
quietly I spread like snow
the silence of my heart,

and discover this day
how deeply I belong.

About the Author

Graduate of the University of Notre Dame, Don had an extensive career in construction management, including major facilities throughout the Pacific Northwest. Author of five volumes of poetry and the online "Poet's Journal," he lives with his wife, artist and glass sculptor Linda Ethier, between the San Juan Islands and Portland Oregon.